2/88

France

Over the past thirty years, France has transformed herself from being a typical post-war European country, inward-looking and jealously proud of her traditions and past, into one of the world's most successful and efficient industrial powers. In spite of the priority, often state-directed, towards the strengthening of France's industrial and agricultural base, the country has retained those characteristics which have always set her apart from her European neighbors – her unfailing sense of style, her passion for good food, her unshakeable but, to foreigners, often infuriating belief in the supremacy of all things French.

In We Live in France, a cross-section of the French people tell you what their life is like – life in industry, life in agriculture, life in France's overcrowded cities.

The author, James Tomlins, works on the English desk of France's news agency, Agence France-Presse, and has lived and worked in Paris for the past fifteen years.

North Sea

THE NETHERLANDS

ENGLAND

WEST GERMANY

BELGIUM

LUXEMBOURG

English Channel

• Cherbourg

• Rouen

Seine

Strasbourg •

Poissy • • Paris

Rennes •

Guebwiller •

Orléans •

Loire

Tours •

Dijon •

Nantes •

SWITZERL

Atlantic Ocean

Limoges •

Lyons

St. Etienne •

Bordeaux •

Rhône

Garonne

Toulouse •

Marseilles

• Narbonne

SPAIN

Mediterranean Sea

we live in
FRANCE

James Tomlins

A Living Here Book

The Bookwright Press
New York · 1983

Living Here

First published in the United States in 1983 by
The Bookwright Press, 387 Park Avenue South,
New York NY 10016
First published in 1982 by
Wayland Publishers Limited, England

ISBN: 0–531–04688–5
Library of Congress Catalog Card Number: 83–71633

Printed by G. Canale & C.S.p.A., Turin, Italy

Contents

"Rules are rules and must be obeyed"

Arianne Douchand, 13, is a pupil at a secondary school in Orleans with 500 boys and girls. Her brother Arnaud, 14, goes to the same school.

I suppose you would say that I'm average – I am fifth in my class of twenty. My report cards always say that I'm too talkative. But I study hard, and discipline is strict. Arnaud was caught fighting with some other boys recently and the headmaster – he is senior to the headmistress – punished him by suspending him for three days. He wouldn't even see my parents about it. They were told rules are rules, and must be obeyed.

We don't wear school uniforms in state schools – only private schools do, and they're terribly expensive. Under a recent educational reform we get all our school textbooks and notebooks, as well as pens and pencils, free of charge. I eat lunch every day in our cafeteria, which has forty tables, with eight places

Wooden desks with inkwells have yet to disappear from this typical French classroom.

at each table.

For lunch today I had a lettuce salad, then roast beef with mashed potatoes followed by two different cheeses and an orange. Of course, you can eat as much bread as you want. No butter. That's in the cooking. We're not allowed to have wine. The school charges 370 francs ($51) a term for school meals.

I live near enough to the school to bicycle to and from home. We work four and a half days a week, starting at 8:00 a.m. and finishing at 4:30 p.m., with a break for lunch. There's no school on Wednesdays.

Today, for instance, I started with one hour of art, followed by one hour of French, then an hour of English and an hour of German. In the afternoon it was all math. I enjoy English and math. Each teacher has a classroom, and we go to the teachers in their rooms, rather than have them coming to us.

As well as classes, we have three hours of sports a week, when we play handball, and volleyball and do gymnastics. Some girls go swimming.

I'm also taking music lessons, learning how to read music and to play the flute. Oddly enough most flutes in France are not made here. They're imported from Japan as the Japanese can make them more cheaply.

Do I use makeup? No, I'm far too young, but many of the older girls do.

There is a problem at some schools with immigrant children. If more than half the class are immigrant children, Arabs or Africans, then the French children are taken away by their parents. My class has only three foreigners – a black from Martinique and two Arabs from North Africa. They're treated just like everybody else. We have no racial prob-

Until recently children had to buy all their own textbooks and notebooks.

lems – the teachers would never allow it.

Have I decided what I want to be when I grow up? Well, there's a lot of schooling for me before that happens. But at the moment I would like to be an actress, so I go to the movies a lot.

My favorite subject is English. This summer my class went on a camping trip to Scotland for two weeks. There are no religious classes – religious instruction in French state schools has been forbidden since the Revolution, when the church and state were separated. I hardly ever go to church; I'm not even baptized.

"Longer hours for less money"

Georges Teste, 52, has been a Paris taxi driver for the past eighteen years. He is looking forward to retiring in a few years as he finds he is having to work longer and longer hours to cope with rising gasoline prices, registration fees and insurance.

It's a long day from 6:00 a.m. to 7:00 p.m., especially in Paris traffic, but I take an hour off at 2:00 p.m. to go home for lunch.

How many taxis would you say there are in Paris? Well, there are 14,500. I have my own private taxi because the big companies have their drivers hooked up to a radio-call circuit, and that would drive me crazy.

I don't have a radio, but rely on clients like you hailing me on the street. I figure I get between fourteen and eighteen clients a day.

I've seen some big changes. Today there are about 3,000 women drivers – there were only a few hundred when I started. Then you've probably noticed a large number of foreign drivers – Asians,

Taxi drivers wait to pick up passengers in the famous Champs Elysées.

Arabs and some black Africans — about 2,000 of them altogether.

I always say that you can tell French history from our taxi drivers. The Asians are refugees from our former Indo-Chinese colonies such as Vietnam, Cambodia and Laos, and the Arabs are from Algeria and Tunisia. The blacks are from French-speaking former African colonies such as Senegal and Mali.

You've probably noticed that many taxi drivers have dogs sitting beside them. There have been cases of drivers being attacked by their passengers, so many taxi drivers now carry guns which fire tear gas, or they have a blackjack. No licenses needed for them. Some of my friends actually have revolvers or pistols, but the police ask too many questions.

But I think it's cruel to keep a dog in a taxi, so I don't. And I'm completely unarmed. If I think that a client may give me trouble, then I refuse to take him. I'm within the law.

And talking about the law, do you know that in all my years as a taxi driver, I've not been given a single traffic ticket for an offense. Not a bad record.

But I am really looking forward to retiring. Traffic jams are getting worse every year, and with rising prices of gasoline, registration fees and insurance, I have to work longer hours for less money.

The radio taxi is a hellish invention; the taxi driver is at the beck and call of his dispatcher every minute of the day. Some of my young colleagues get sick and have to leave the profession completely. You never hear of them again.

These days taxi companies put no-smoking notices in their vehicles, but I don't. I let clients relax and have a cigarette in comfort, although personally I am a nonsmoker.

My philosophy in life is that at my age I'm not ambitious. I just want to take things easy. No more quick self-service snacks. I go home for lunch. Today for instance I started with an *hors d'oeuvre* of pâté with radishes, then yesterday's reheated veal stew cooked in white wine with mushroom sauce, then goat's cheese and bread and a fresh apple, washed down with inexpensive wine.

I believe in keeping relaxed and healthy. I've inherited a house which overlooks the Pyrenees — I go there every year.

I also have an allotment near my home just outside Paris, and I grow flowers there. My real passion is for roses. That's what I think about as I drive around Paris all day — fields and fields of roses.

Heavy traffic during the Paris rush hour makes life difficult for drivers and passengers alike.

"Our main enemy is indifference"

Abbé Jean Laverton, 31, is one of four Catholic priests in the parish of Saint Jacques, one of the ninety parishes in Paris. His congregation is growing smaller: he attributes this to the lack of faith shown by many young people and to the indifference of their parents.

There can be no doubt that there is a lack of faith among ordinary people in the country. It's even becoming difficult recruiting enough priests. Take our parish as an example. Twenty years ago we could count on 24,000 worshipers, while today we have only 18,000. A drop of twenty-five percent. Most French people are baptized Catholics, but only about ten to fifteen percent of them are active worshipers. How many people do you think attend confession each month? About eight. There have been many changes in the past fifteen years or so. People don't see confession in the same way as they used to. Many find it difficult.

Elderly parishioners who are active Catholics tell me they can do nothing to make their grandchildren go to church regularly.

Despite its central location, St. Jacques church attracts fewer and fewer worshipers.

Our total congregation at various services on the Sabbath is about 1,200. And we're located in a heavily built-up area of the capital.

The St. Jacques church has a lot of expenses with baptisms, funerals and various charitable works, as well as paying the four clergy, but our annual budget is a mere million francs ($140,000). Cardinal Marty of Paris has urged Catholics to give one percent of their income to the church. One percent. It's little, but very few people are prepared to give it.

The reason is sheer indifference. That's our main enemy — indifference. I believe it stems from a high living standard and material comfort. In the 1968 student riots in Paris graffiti were painted on the walls reading "God is dead," but that intense hostility is over. We're faced with Catholics who just don't care.

I became a priest because I did care — from the age of seven, according to my parents. I knew it was my vocation. I spent five years in Rome and returned to Paris in 1977 when I was ordained a priest. I was twenty-nine then.

I joined this parish two years ago, and I look after the young people here. We have a scout movement, and we also organize discussions and outings. But our youth movement is relatively small — about sixty. You can imagine the other temptations for young people in a big city like this.

I have other duties, such as caring for the needy, like tramps. They need food, clothing and money. And then people come and tell us tall stories to get money. I suppose they think we're rich.

Some priests tell me that our young people are more intelligent than the youth of thirty years ago. They know

The cathedral of Notre Dame is considered more of a tourist attraction than a place of worship.

more about the world and can discuss foreign affairs and current events. But they lack a system of thought, a coherent structure on which to build their lives. Briefly, they lack faith. That's why I'm a priest — to give it to them. It will be a lifetime's work for me.

"There's nothing better than hard work"

Emile Delbouis, 48, owns a small but flourishing bistro. Born in the Auvergne region, he received little education and has had to put in years of hard work to build up his business. He is not optimistic about the future of bistros.

I work fifteen hours a day, sometimes more, in a smoke-filled atmosphere, always running from one customer to another; so you may well ask why did you become a bistro owner?

I was poor and uneducated, like most of those born in the Auvergne region, in the mountainous French Midi. There are about 10,000 bistros in Paris and 80 per-cent of the owners come from the Auvergne. Like me they had no training, no career. They could only be waiters.

My two strong arms and good health have been my mainstays. I haven't spent one day ill in bed for the past twenty

It's more expensive but more fun to take your refreshment at a sidewalk table.

years; six days a week I open my bistro at 6:00 a.m. and close at 8:30 or 9:30 p.m. There are no licensing laws in this country, so we keep open until the last customer leaves.

I bought my bistro twenty-two years ago and for the first seven years my wife and I never took a vacation. We went without things to build up a stock of drinks.

There are six other bistros within a three-minute walk of mine, so you can see the kind of competition there is. But I've built up my own regular customers, mainly students from the Law Faculty down the road or the Faculty of Architecture next door. Then there's the hospital just opposite where the singer Charles Aznavour was born. So I'm kept busy.

What do they drink? A lot of *pastis* and *Ricard* (aniseed-tasting apéritifs), Calvados (alcohol made from apples), rum, and a lot of red wine. Cognac is too expensive and my whiskey sales are zero. It may surprise you, but a lot of my customers buy water. I'm not joking. Yes, water! It's bottled mineral water like *Evian*, which is still, or *Perrier*, which is fizzy. I bet not many foreigners will believe that!

I also prepare snacks like frankfurters with french fries, and what we call a *croque-monsieur*, which is a toasted ham-and-cheese sandwich. They're very filling and good value for hungry students.

Customers can stay in the bistro for hours over one small coffee, reading the newspapers, or if they are students, doing their homework.

Yes, *bistro* is a funny name. It dates from 1815 when Russian officers accompanied Czar Alexander II to Paris after the Battle of Waterloo when Napoleon

The larger, modern cafés are posing a threat to the traditional bistros of France.

was defeated. These officers were always rushing into our cafés for a quick drink and shouting *bistr*, which in Russian means "hurry." The word stuck.

You see that crescent-shaped bun there, a *croissant*? Well that's supposed to be as French as the Eiffel Tower, but, you know, it really came from Vienna. We French are always willing to take ideas from foreigners, especially if they're good ones.

I can't see much future for the bistro. Young people are no longer prepared to work the long, killing hours. You see, Monsieur, they're better educated; they want something better. For me there's nothing better than plain, hard work.

"The client must come first"

Gérard Voillaume, 30, is a receptionist in a three-star hotel in the heart of old Paris, much frequented by French provincial visitors. He has seen big changes in the pattern of tourism over the past ten years, but insists that Paris is still a city everyone wants to visit.

France welcomes over 15 million foreign visitors every year, but the statistics often forget the several million Frenchmen and women who travel about their own country on business or for pleasure. We have ninety-eight beds and half our clientele is foreign and half, French.

We get a lot of German visitors. Some of them who are middle-aged admit they were last here during the war, as part of the army of Occupation. They didn't dare come back before, but you know, the war might have been 100 years ago now. All that is forgotten. That's what I like about this hotel business – you meet so many different kinds of people. I'm well-equipped because I speak three foreign languages – English, German and Spanish.

My career has followed a logical path. I wanted to go into the hotel–restaurant business ever since I was eleven and a waiter served my parents and me wearing white gloves. You don't see that very much these days – that's real style.

What tourist could fail to be moved by the beauty of Montmartre's Sacre Coeur?

I left school at seventeen and for the next three years I attended special hotel–restaurant courses. I worked in the kitchen where I was a *marmiton* – that's someone who scours pots and pans. It's the lowest rank in our business, even lower than a dishwasher, and it's heavy, dirty work. Then I became a chef's assistant. You've never seen a bad-tempered man, until you've seen a chef conjure up 100 dishes for a banquet and then something goes wrong.

I read the other day that there's one leading woman chef in France – just one among thousands of men. The reason is women can't stand the tension and frustrations of work in the kitchen with all these *prima donnas* such as headwaiters, wine waiters, and table managers as well as hungry, impatient and tired customers.

From the kitchen I graduated to the restaurant – I even wore white gloves when serving. Believe me, you have to work long hours, and you must be really fit. Then I went to the *cave*, or cellar, where the wines are stored. There you learn the mysteries of wine in three months – or try to, but of course it would really take a lifetime.

My next move was to the accounting department, where I learned how to check room, bar and restaurant bills. Then I completed my course as a receptionist at several big hotels before coming here at the age of twenty. I have been here ever since.

There have been big changes in the last ten years in the numbers and nationalities of tourists. But Paris is one of those cities people want to see at least once in their lives, whatever the cost.

When visitors arrive here – from

The symbol of Paris. Elegant or vulgar, the Eiffel Tower is top of the tourists' sightseeing list.

abroad or the provinces – the first trip they make is to see the Eiffel Tower. Then the Louvre. Then the Folies Bergère. The pattern has never changed, ever since the hotel opened in 1919.

Sadly Paris, the city of light, is beginning to go dim in some parts. The Latin Quarter, the Champs-Elysées and Pigalle are still lively all through the night until dawn, but other parts of the capital are dead after 8:00 p.m. Maybe it's because of television, or perhaps people are saving money for weekend trips or winter skiing.

Yes, we're taught that the client must come first. I don't say they are always right, but we must let them think they are. The receptionist's greatest virtue is self-control. Like the long hours, it's hard sometimes.

15

"The young neglect their teeth"

Dr. Robert Fromentin has been a dental surgeon for a quarter of a century. He fears that, despite television advertising and regular visits by school dentists, young people are not aware of the need for strict oral hygiene.

Tremendous progress has been made in dentistry this century, particularly in the years just after the last war. But despite all the modern equipment, which can cost a dentist up to 100,000 francs ($14,000), I've always maintained that the most useful item costs a mere ten francs ($1.40). It's a toothbrush. Recently we held a congress here. Of course there had to be a delegate making newspaper headlines by saying that there was no need in these modern days for children to brush their teeth. But he is totally wrong. There's no better way known to science to keep teeth clean and strong.

Over the last twenty years French people have become more interested in their teeth for many reasons. They spend a lot of money on repairing their cars so why not invest in their own health, especially teeth. People don't realize the tremendous power exerted by jaw muscles when they chew, munch and eat. All this strains and puts pressures on those white ivory things called teeth. I shouldn't

have thought it was too much to ask people to have a checkup twice a year.

That man who has just walked out has just completed twelve visits during which I took out six teeth and gave him two dental plates. My bill was about

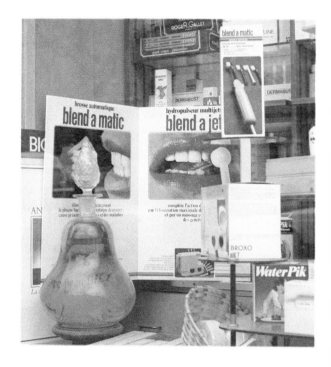

Rich French food is no friend to the teeth, but eating habits are changing even in France.

4,000 francs ($550). Mind you, his mouth was a ruin when he came to me, not having been to a dentist for ten years. He was reduced to eating mashed food and hadn't eaten meat for several years. That's what I mean about a man neglecting to invest in himself.

Unfortunately, there's a widespread lack of oral hygiene among young people, despite the fact that the State pays for television advertising about it.

Recently, an inventor marketed what he called a musical toothbrush, which played several tunes when teeth were brushed up and down, the right way, but became silent when the teeth were brushed horizontally, the wrong way. Any gimmick is worth having if children will only brush their teeth regularly.

But they must also care for their gums, a very neglected part of the mouth.

Any gimmick that will encourage oral hygiene is welcomed by the dentist.

Every term a dentist visits schools to check teeth and give them a thorough overhaul if needed.

French food is so rich in sauces and creams that I'm amazed there are any teeth left in people over thirty. Diet must have an effect on the calcium content of teeth. Wrong food means below-normal calcium, and that means poor teeth.

I work here through the week except Thursdays; then I lecture to dental students. Incidentally, there are far too many wanting to enter the profession, so we have to give tough entry examinations.

But I don't think people should grumble when they're better off than kings were centuries ago. Just look how the "Sun King," Louis XIV, ate meat in his last few years with a metal instrument that looked like a nutcracker. Or Empress Catherine the Great of Russia — she lost all her teeth long before she died.

But then, perhaps as princes and princesses, nobody could tell them to brush their teeth.

"Everybody seems against you"

Soraya Elhadjene, 18, is unemployed and has been vainly seeking work ever since she left school in Saint-Etienne six months ago. There seemed little chance of her securing a job in her hometown, so she tried Paris.

Many young people are jobless like me. We all knew that finding a job, any job, would be difficult. But we never imagined it would be as bad as I have found it for the past six months. It's so discouraging to spend the whole day walking about Paris, answering advertisements. I don't think that I've ever been so tired.

I'm registered with the National Employment Agency, but my home is in Saint-Etienne, near Lyons, where the big firm Manufrance has just closed down, making over 1,500 people jobless. There's not much hope of finding a job in that area now.

I came to Paris a month ago: I thought there would be more opportunities in the capital. But it's a killing process. I've just

More and more young people are forced to seek jobs through employment bureaus.

left school and I'm not entitled to unemployment benefits as I haven't worked three months. But how do they expect you to have worked when you've just left school?

Yesterday I put a two-line advertisement in the main evening newspaper, *France-Soir*, which cost me 56 francs for just one appearance. But I still have no job. I read four newspapers a day studying the job vacancy columns, and then rush off to apply. It's no good telephoning. Last week I missed a job literally by one minute. My bus was held up and when I got to the office a girl had arrived just in front of me, and got the job.

Young people have so many dreams and hopes at school. My ambition is to go into the theater, but as I have no job, I have no money to spend on taking an acting course.

I feel I'm enterprising and imaginative. I went to England twice to work as an au-pair girl, and I was very happy there. But that kind of job is only temporary.

Nothing can be so tiring as trudging a Paris pavement. The whole city seems to be made of extra-hard concrete. And in ice-cold weather, the pavements are slippery and dangerous as well.

Somehow when you're out of work, everything and everybody seems against you. I know it's not really true, but it seems so. Even though I'm young, I get depressed. Some young people even commit suicide.

But you just have to keep on knocking at closed doors and hoping they'll open. At the moment I'm trying to get a job as a salesgirl, as there seem to be more openings there, or in a dress shop.

I have a friend with an arts degree who wants to teach, but she's working as a cleaning woman. A cleaning woman!

It is often harder for an immigrant to find a job than it is for a French person.

That's the world today. You must lower your expectations if you want to survive.

When you've just left school, you will only receive unemployment benefits if you have a technical trade certificate. Otherwise nothing. And you must hold down your first job for three months before you're entitled to unemployment benefits.

The ranks of the unemployed are growing in France – they have doubled in the past seven years.

There are political repercussions, but they are cushioned by the fact that the economic recession is worldwide, so no one French political party can be blamed.

One unfortunate result of high unemployment is that foreign immigrants – there are two million Arabs, Africans, Spanish, Portuguese and Yugoslavs in France – suffer the most when a firm starts cutting down on its staff.

19

"French law is realistic"

Gérard Bernardi is a *commissaire principal* (chief inspector) in the Interior Ministry with 24 years' service. He echoes a growing concern among French people about their personal security: people no longer feel safe in the streets of Paris at night.

A police officer experiences many bad moments in his career. I've always thought the most dangerous part of a policeman's job involves dealing with armed madmen. Once I had to cope with just such a situation when a man rushed at me with an axe. I was much younger and tougher in those days and managed to overpower him. But it was frightening, because you can't reason with madmen.

People forget that a large part of police work is being able to persuade a criminal to surrender. Some years ago, when I was a *commissaire* in a Paris suburb, a gunman walked into a local *bistro* and shot his wife's boyfriend in front of a dozen witnesses. They identified the killer and I went to the man's father and spent all night persuading him that his

Crime is not the policeman's only concern. He also has to perform mundane tasks such as this.

Marie-Antoinette was once held prisoner in the fourteenth-century conciergerie.

son must surrender to us. When the son telephoned about dawn and heard what his father had to say, he gave himself up. So a murder was solved, and the murderer arrested and duly tried. No, he was not executed.

We have what we call the *crime passionnel* (crime of passion) in France, which is always punished less harshly. These crimes come about when men and women are caught up in powerful emotion caused by passion, which turns them into killers. When the emotion is spent, the person becomes normal. French law is realistic and recognizes this. Just look at the latest available murder figures for France in one year. They're divided into two classes – murder for profit or for some vicious motive (29), and murder for passion (327).

A murderer motivated by passion has never been guillotined in France, but we're accused of being bloodthirsty because we're the only country in Western Europe to keep the death penalty. Only six men have been guillotined in the past ten years. The guillotine is only used for really terrible crimes like killing a child or a prison guard, or for a kidnap-murder. Personally, I'm against the death penalty, but most police are for it, and I believe the majority of French people want to keep it.

It reflects a growing concern about personal security. In Paris there were 44,000 burglaries of private homes and apartments in 1979 – or five every hour. But people are more worried about being attacked in the streets at night. That's what people come to the police about, really shaken.

So we're seeing an increase in the number of people buying guns to defend themselves or forming little private militias. Recently three shopkeepers who each killed a burglar in separate incidents were found not guilty of any crime and released.

But police have other things to do besides fighting crime. We have to control the traffic and deal with street demonstrations. At the moment I'm talking to you, there are three demonstrations going on in Paris, and they have to be controlled by experienced men. We have a specially-trained unit to do this, just as we have a special squad to guard foreign V.I.P.s.

As for traffic, we lead the world in methods of keeping the traffic moving by the use of one-way streets, and special lanes for buses and taxis, which run against the main stream of the traffic.

We were able to do this because Paris is fortunate in having wide avenues and boulevards.

Incidentally, all foreigners think of us as *gendarmes*. But the police force and *gendarmerie* are quite different bodies. The *gendarmerie* is a militarized state police, and it even has tanks. *Gendarmes* are like troops, living in barracks. Police take off their uniforms when they are home and wear civilian clothes.

But look at me. I wear civilian clothes even when I'm working. Yet we're all police.

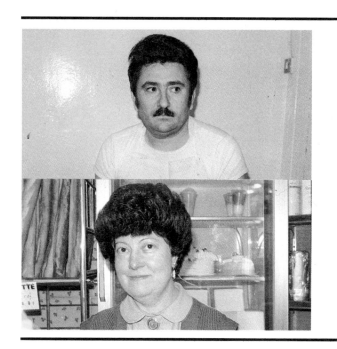

"There's no bread like French bread"

Jack and Andrée Richer own a bakery in Paris. Traditional French bread is renowned for its high quality, but small bakers are threatened by the increased popularity of cheaper, and inferior, mass-produced bread.

Nobody makes bread like we French bakers, and I'm not just boasting. The English and Americans have all tried, but they can't make fresh, crusty *baguettes* like we do. Nor the breakfast *croissant* for that matter. It's partly the higher quality of our white flour and our rich French soil, but it's also the baker's art and craft.

Yet we're a dying race, we bakers. There are fewer and fewer of us each year. In Paris, for example, there are at present 1,700 bakers, but they are closing down at a rate of seventy-five a year. By the year 2000, there will only be a few hundred of us left.

There are several reasons for this. Did you know that French people eat less bread these days than their fathers did? That's a fact.

In the '50s, when I was doing my three-year apprenticeship, a family would buy three *baguettes*. Each *baguette* weighs 250 grams (9 oz) — that made a total consumption of 750 grams (1 lb 11 oz) of bread a day.

Nowadays a family buys one *baguette* a day. One reason is that the standard of living has risen and people are eating

A *shopper walks home with a week-end's supply of* baguettes.

more meat and vegetables instead of filling themselves up with bread, even excellent bread like ours.

Another main reason is that bakers' sons no longer follow their father's trade as they did before the war. This is partly because we work such long hours, which spoils any social life in the evenings.

My bakery has four furnace periods, each running for three to four hours, starting at 4:00 a.m. There are seven of us in all, including two apprentices, my wife, and the store clerks. Sometimes we serve up to 1,000 clients a day in the shop. Then we have other customers including three bistros and a large school.

Industrialization is my main worry; it's slowly stealing my big customers. I've already lost two big customers, a nearby hospital and school. They prefer to buy mass-produced bread made in a faraway factory, because it's cheaper.

There are nineteen different shapes of

In France, even the most basic foods can appear to be a luxury.

French loaf and the idea is that you choose them according to the dish you are eating them with. They're shaped by hand – not put in a mold. As our dough doesn't contain any chemical products, the bread goes stale quicker and can't be kept overnight.

I've never regretted becoming a baker. My father was a civil servant who saw that I was getting nowhere at what I wanted to .do – commercial designing. He said that I must get a trade, and apprenticed me to a baker. Then I did thirty months military service in Algeria, married Andrée and opened my own shop in Tours. I was there for seven years and then came here twelve years ago.

It's a good living and I still design – chocolate rabbits and fish for Easter, and Santa Clauses for Christmas. They make a colorful display in the window. They're expensive and I don't sell many. I don't mind. I do it for my own pleasure.

"Parents lack interest in education"

Jean-Pierre Hammel, 59, is the Vice-Principal of the École Alsacienne, Paris, a school with 1,450 pupils. He sees in the children he teaches a lack of confidence in the future, which he attributes to their fear of another war.

I came here thirty-two years ago, in 1948, and have never thought of going anywhere else. It's the top as far as I'm concerned. From the street, nobody would guess that there is a thriving school here as large as a village. We take pupils from the age of four to sixteen years and have about 100 teachers. We're a private day-school, founded in 1874, and our fees are 1,500 francs ($200) per term. But the State pays the teaching staff.

I suppose you could say that discipline is firm here – although we don't have school uniforms – and we haven't expelled a pupil for ten years. Incidentally, I'm in charge of discipline. There's no corporal punishment. We just exclude pupils from school for one to three days. If this doesn't work, then we try persuasion by talking with the pupil, his or her friends, and of course parents.

Yes, there are problems. I've seen a big change in pupils over the past fifteen years. The previous generation was more aggressive and ready to argue, always questioning authority. This spirit led to

Behind this unimposing exterior lies a school as large as a village.

Much of a teacher's time is taken up with preparing lessons for the following day.

the May 1968 student riots in Paris. Today our pupils show a lack of confidence in their future. It's quite marked. Mass communication – newspapers, radio and television – are hammering out frightening news such as the invasion of Afghanistan or the Iraq–Iran War or the Middle East crisis or Poland. Children are faced with the prospect of another world war.

So far as levels of intelligence are concerned, there is little difference between the generations. Pocket calculators, television and computers have not had any real effect, good or bad, on our pupils. But I can see changes coming.

I would like to give more time to sports – once we had our own fields, until they were built on. Only two hours a week are given to sports – team games and gymnastics. No football or rugby, because we don't have sports fields. We have a courtyard, but this is obviously hardly enough for our real needs.

Our examination results are usually the best in France – ninety-four percent successes this year, for instance. We are strong on languages, mainly English and German, but also Spanish, Italian, Chinese, Russian and Hebrew. At one time in France the teaching of Latin and Greek started to drop off, but today it's on the increase again. We teach both here.

Our most difficult age group is fourteen to sixteen years. We have mixed classes, but at this age the girls are really women, and the boys are still children.

In some ways our main problem is what happens outside school – in the home of our pupils. We don't feel that parents are interested enough in the whole process of education. But then that's an almost international complaint these days.

Everybody who visits us notices that there's an air of learning about us; it stretches from the top to the bottom. When our janitor man, Jacques Peyraud, left us recently, he wrote us a superb poem which we published in our monthly magazine.

"Opening up windows on the world"

Solange Lhuilier is a senior civil servant working in a section of the Postal and Telecommunications Ministry (PTT) at the Bureau Télégraphique International, Paris. She deals with telex messages sent all over the world.

I started working here in 1962. In those days there were only a couple of us handling overseas telegrams and just a few telexes. Today most of our communications are sent by telex and the telegram is reserved for contacting remote countries like North Yemen. Ten years ago we had to call up foreign operators and ask them to forward our message, but two years ago the system was automated, which means we can call numbers direct. Once a person has used the telex system he is unlikely to go back to using the telephone or airmail letters. The telex is a written record of your communication, which a telephone conversation is not. Telexes are also cheaper. A transcontinental telex call costs 20 francs ($2.75) per minute compared to 25 francs ($3.50) for a telephone call. Another advantage is that nobody can ignore a telex message. It just demands to be answered promptly.

France's new shortwave radio transmitter for telexes.

You hear a lot about France's 2 million civil servants complaining about their jobs, but I'm really happy at my work. I start at 7:00 p.m. and finish at midnight. During that time I like to think I'm opening up windows on the world as I dial Peking, Washington or Johannesburg.

Over half our messages are sent by journalists. It can be difficult when we have to tap out a message that a Japanese has written out in his own characters and then transcribed into Latin letters.

After all, we're responsible for total accuracy, and checking what is an incomprehensible message to us is difficult.

But the attraction of foreign places is always with us in our work. My husband also works in the telecommunications side of the PTT, and my sixteen-year-old son is studying electronics before joining the PTT as well.

My husband and I spent three years in Mali – a former French African colony – helping them to organize and run their telecommunication services. But life there was hard. There were food shortages and, as my children were much younger – one was a baby – we had to send to France for their needs. But you still get many French technicians going to Africa as cooperation advisers. We train Africans here in telecommunications and then find they're unwilling to return home because they earn so little there and the equipment needs constant repairing. So the PTT employs them here.

We transmit in every known language but funnily enough never in Russian. Most of us read English, German, Spanish and Italian. Sometimes a press correspondent wants to play truant, so he sends a telex to say there's been a Post Office strike for two days and therefore he has been unable to phone or telex reports. Or he blames us for a lengthy delay when really he'd been late giving his telex in. Sometimes you get deadly enemies working shoulder to shoulder, like a South African journalist beside an African. Once two Asians gave us their telexes and then one asked for his back again. He was given the other man's by mistake. There was almost a fight – one was from North Korea (Pyongyang) and

These new glass telephone booths are springing up all over France.

the other from South Korea (Seoul). But as their governments have no diplomatic relations, neither Korean dared to speak to the other. They just glared furiously.

The French Telephone system has made immense progress. Ten years ago, it was ranked eighteenth in Europe. Today it is fifth in the world regarding telephones per head of population, after U.S., Japan, Britain and West Germany. There are 16 million main lines compared with 11 million in 1978, and the system is fully automatic to 140 countries.

There are over 80,000 telex subscribers, and they're increasing by leaps and bounds.

The Post Office accounts for a large proportion of state expenditure, for it employs over 830,000 people.

"People have changed their eating habits"

Georges Constant, 57, is one of France's foremost chefs; he runs "Chez Georges". Cooking is not his only task — he also has to buy the supplies for the kitchen, select the wines, and receive his customers.

I've been a chef since I was a boy. I went to a school for chefs and served as an apprentice. My father was a chef and so was my grandfather. And my son-in-law is also a chef. Four generations of chefs in one family. Quite a record.

My grandfather opened his own restaurant, quite near here, in 1912. My father and I both worked there. Mind you, I never look on cooking as work. It means long hours, but I would never want to do anything else.

But remember that running a restaurant is not just being a chef. I have to manage my staff, buy the food, select wines and, perhaps most important of all, deal with the customers who come here.

A chef has to be a psychologist too. He

A chef must not only cook well. He also has to buy the best provisions for his kitchen.

must make his customers feel comfortable, and help them choose their dishes without bullying them. I spend much of my time in the kitchen or out buying things, but as soon as the first customer walks through the door I am in the restaurant.

We're old-fashioned here. Look at the menu. I write it out by hand on a piece of paper with a special ink on the back. The inked side is pressed onto a soft clay-like substance which acts as a mold and then I make as many menus as we need. We're one of the few restaurants to use this process, which was passed down by my grandfather. The menu for today is: casserole of snails; a thick slice of duck's breast, with mushroom sauce; *tarte tatin*, an apple dessert; Beaujolais 1980; price – seventy francs ($9.70).

I print up a new menu every day. So we don't have the same dishes week after week like many modern restaurants that print their menus by machine. We change the main dishes every day.

Our busiest time is from noon to 3:00 p.m. when we serve lunch and from 7:30 in the evening when we serve dinner. We don't accept any customers after 9:30 p.m., but those who arrive before then can stay until midnight. Meals should never be rushed.

I have three chefs and two apprentices. All my chefs are men, as in most restaurants in France. Women can cook well – they are more careful workers – but I think they work better at home, where there's less pressure than here.

My restaurant seats sixty people. I employ only waitresses, no male waiters. Most of our customers are men and they appreciate the feminine touch.

Yes, eating habits have changed in the past ten years or so. We serve much more

The early-morning scene the customer never sees.

grilled food, nowadays, probably because it's less fattening and customers are more conscious of weight problems. They also want something that is easy to digest. We also serve much more fish than we used to, especially expensive fish like turbot or sole.

You can't become a chef in less than seven years as you have to know so much and gain practical experience. In France, which worships food like no other nation except perhaps China, the chef enjoys a very high status in society, higher than in any other country in the world. We don't work in a kitchen: we create art in a *cuisine*.

My greatest pleasure as chef is not working in my kitchen – it's choosing the wines. I go directly to the producer for them and taste them myself.

"Industrial espionage in Toyland"

Monique Lemoine, 49, inherited the family stationery store her grandfather opened in 1910. She has modernized the business and now specializes in toys. French toy manufacturers are being hit by the import of cheap goods.

Yes, everybody says how much younger I look than my age. I put it down to all the toys I handle. In my father's and grandfather's day, the store sold paper, pens and erasers, but I have modernized the shop and also sell electronic games, puzzles and all sorts of gadgets, as well as watches and pocket calculators.

I was born here, so I know the area and people well. Fortunately I live just above my store, so there's no tiring journey to and from work. As a child, I used to help my father in the store, which was a classic stationery of those times. I inherited it from him when he died in 1962, and continued the business more or less as it was, but decided on a radical change in 1968, the year of the student riots.

People come here to buy expensive-looking presents at a cheap price. Many of the presents are totally useless, but cheer people up. A miniature guillotine was popular, but toy alcohol-test kits never sold. I have to buy stock six months in advance and try to gauge what will interest my customers.

On the stationery side I find that fewer Christmas cards are being bought. People prefer to use the telephone to send greetings, even if it is to the United States or Japan. Funny to think that the improvement in the telephone system has affected my business.

We still sell a lot of visiting cards, but then the French people have always been great ones for using them. This custom has by no means died out; in fact, I think it's increasing. Even young people want their own visiting cards. We even print them on thin sheets of Japanese wood — the last word in elegance.

It's a pity that so many people don't realize how many varied items I stock here. The store is so tiny and many things are stacked on shelves and can't be seen.

But I love small things. Look at this tiny miniature music box which plays Brahms' *Lullaby*. Only 26 francs ($3.60), and we should sell thousands but few people know they are here.

You know each year I come to the conclusion that there are no more toys to invent. But no, new toys still come rolling out of the factories.

Of course, it's big business. At Christmas, the French spend millions of francs on toys, but only half of the toys they buy are made in France. There are only 300

No school, no toys, but still the children manage to amuse themselves.

A veritable treasure chest confronts the visitor to Monique's little store.

toy-making factories compared with 500 in 1970. We have been invaded by foreign toys.

Let me tell you a true story. At the beginning of every year, French toy manufacturers hold a trade fair to show their newest lines. The public isn't allowed in. This year, one of the officials saw three Asians take a model truck, about eight inches long, and then photograph it about 100 times, from every angle. He stopped them and called the security guards. They were South Koreans, and one was a diplomat from their embassy in Paris. The other two were businessmen, and they planned to make millions of these trucks and sell them cheaply. A real case of industrial espionage in Toyland.

Sometimes I wonder if modern toys are really better than those we had in the old days. I've seen a doll with its own visiting cards engraved in its own name – Madeleine – and with a dozen dresses and its own miniature furniture. That's what little girls were being bought – in 1867.

"We aren't taken seriously"

Jean-Pierre Bousquet, 39, is a professional journalist with France's news agency, Agence France-Presse. He had wanted to become a professor of Spanish, but he realizes that journalism is his true profession.

We say in France that a journalist is usually somebody who failed in his first choice of a career. Like me. I wanted to be a professor of Spanish, but I could only obtain a scholarship to continue studying if I signed on to teach at a state school for ten years. Well, that seemed a lifetime, so I left Narbonne in the south of France where I was born, and went to Paris; I was twenty-one. The classic story of a boy from the provinces going to the big city in search of fame and fortune.

I worked as a journalist on an illustrated Catholic publication for children and continued studying Spanish. Two years later I was called up into the army, and I was the first journalist to be sent overseas as part of France's program of cooperation and aid to its former

A customer at a newsstand is rarely stuck for choice.

There's always a spare moment when you can stop and catch up on the news.

colonies throughout the world.

I did my military service in the Republic of Niger, a landlocked country twice the size of France. I spent eighteen months there, helping their Ministry of Information. In 1966 I returned to Paris and spent the next six months looking for a job.

I went to Dijon in central France to work as sports editor on the daily newspaper *Le Bien Public*. This is one of France's oldest newspapers, with a circulation of 50,000.

I returned to Paris in 1969 and spent the next two years working on the magazine *Architecture-Construction Mécanique*. A journalist has to turn his hand to every subject. Then I joined Agence France-Presse (A.F.P.).

I married and settled down to working on the night shift on A.F.P.'s foreign desk for the next four years or so, continuing to study Spanish, and specializing in the economy of Latin America.

In 1975 I was sent to Buenos Aires, capital of Argentina, as a foreign correspondent for A.F.P. – the ambition of every newsman.

What's the difference between being a correspondent and a reporter? Well, we jokingly say "about a hundred and sixty dollars a week."

You know, to speak another language and live in another country is to become another person. At the end of my four-year term, I was called back to the head office in Paris for a stint there, but I'll be sent back to Latin America again, or perhaps to Spain.

I've often wondered whether journalists have a very high status in France. Probably not. Our problem is that we aren't taken seriously. But we mustn't act as though we're pundits or philosophers or preachers. Our duty is to hunt, find, write and report news.

I'm writing a book – of course, every journalist is writing a book – but mine will be published, I'm certain.

Other people look at us with envy, and there's much ignorance about what we really do. The best journalists are usually those who don't have a university degree. Our work requires something else: intelligence, intuition, an eye for the telling detail, and sympathy. Lots of sympathy.

Do I regret not becoming a professor? Never. Once you're a journalist, you realize one thing – it's the only job in the world.

"Office work burdens have vanished"

Ghislaine Garnier has worked for the past eight years as a secretary with an international company in Marseilles. She has a university degree in literature but believes that she could not use this qualification to earn her living.

The status of the secretary in France has gone down in the past ten years, but at the same time salaries have gone up. We seem to do more jobs than we used to, and less typing and dictation. We're more specialized, and that's why we get more money. But somehow we seem to have slipped down the social scale. Perhaps because we're looked on as doing too many things, like flight attendants who have also lost status.

Next to my desk I now have a telex machine, which is used so much between countries that it has cut down our letter writing. The French telephone system has improved so much that this also cuts down on the amount of mail we send. These days people are more willing to talk business on the telephone. Once a secretary had to have shorthand, but I'm not sure this is the case today — bosses like to use dictaphones.

In fact, a woman today has to be good at using, and sometimes repairing, gadgets like electric typewriters, rather than keeping her eyes glued to her notebook.

The European Common Market has brought in a lot of new secretarial methods and of course more foreign work. The work is much more interesting, and you don't feel you're in a rut.

My working day starts at 8:30 a.m. and I usually arrive with the mail. We have a

second delivery at 3:30 p.m. The mail is speedy and we figure on getting a letter delivered anywhere in France within twenty-four hours, and within forty-eight hours anywhere in Western Europe.

My work, like that of many senior secretaries, is more that of a coordinator and organizer. This is essential for a company. There may well be many mechanical improvements in offices, but no machine can do these things. There used to be a trend in France for managing directors to have well-dressed male secretaries, but this fashion seems to have died out. They were never called secretaries, of course, but advisers or associates.

Until a few years ago, we worked on Saturday mornings, but this has largely disappeared. This means that more and

No work on Saturdays, so it's off for the weekend with the family.

To a large extent, modern machinery has replaced the secretary's notepad.

more secretaries like me can get away for weekends in the country and return refreshed for our work in the office during the week.

But the old burden of office work has largely vanished, probably because offices have been modernized, with more comfortable chairs and desks and better lighting. There are even pictures on the walls, and sometimes plants and flowers in window boxes. Office life has become more human.

I have a university degree in literature, like thousands of other women, but only a few people are able to make a living from literary work as full-time authors. Most work in bookshops or libraries. I prefer an office. You never know what will turn up. Just a minute, there's the telex machine working. New York on the line. Now what can they want?

" There's always work for a cobbler"

Auguste Attal, 40, is a self-employed cobbler. Although changing fashions and the increased use of man-made materials in shoes are cutting back on the work of cobblers, he is setting up his son in the same business.

I'm one of the few Frenchmen who knows that Napoleon was talking nonsense when he said that an army marches on its stomach – it marches on leather. The shoe trade has tried to find cheaper substitutes, but without success. We have a saying: "Gilding wears out with time and bad weather, but leather endures; there is nothing like leather."

Perhaps that's why leather prices have soared 400 percent in the past four years, although recently they've begun to stabilize.

I like being a cobbler. You're not badgered by someone giving orders from above. And I get real pleasure in cutting and shaping leather with tools, and making battered footwear as good as new.

I started as an ordinary worker in a

The fashion for non-repairable shoes has had a bad effect on the cobbler's business.

factory in Paris. After a couple of years I'd learned every aspect of shoemaking and repairing, and so I opened my own little shop.

All I needed were a few small sewing and cutting machines, and of course my own skill and labor. Today my business is flourishing and I have about 100 customers a day.

I also offer a key-cutting service, which takes just three minutes, but most of my work is repairing footwear. Seventy percent of my customers are women and thirty percent are men. I also make sandals. Shoes are too difficult as I don't have the backup equipment, although I know how to make them.

My shop is open from 9:30 a.m. to 7:30 p.m. five days a week. The work can be hard, especially in winter, when everybody is in a hurry, and soles and heels must be replaced as quickly as possible.

Fifteen years ago I specialized in repair-while-you-wait, in the days when women's shoes had stiletto heels that never lasted more than a week. Those were the good old days. Women's shoe fashions have changed a great deal. Today the fashion is a wide, flatter heel with a simple design – elegant but not ostentatious.

Can you tell a person's character from the shoes he wears? In the old days, perhaps, when many people wore handmade shoes made to their own order. But a handmade shoe in France today is a rarity. Everything is mass-produced in a factory.

That's why we cobblers are needed. You never hear of an unemployed cobbler. There's always work for him. Nevertheless, our craft is a dying one, although I can't see how we will be replaced. Not yet at any rate, so I've trained my son Thierry to follow in my footsteps and I'm buying him his own repair shop.

After all, it pays well, and we cobblers live well. I take a month's vacation in the summer. I've visited Tunisia and the United States – and I take a week's skiing vacation in the winter. I close my shop then, so my customers have to wear out their shoe leather looking for another cobbler.

We're competing with cheap imports from the Far East – they're throwaway shoes not meant to be repaired. They cost about one-third the price of a new French or Italian shoe.

Italian imports are another danger, even though they're more expensive than French shoes. But they're well cut and elegant and use a finer leather.

One depressing influence is the effect made by the cheap linen jogging shoe which many people wear throughout the day. So they don't need a cobbler.

The cobbler still relies on traditional tools in the practice of his craft.

"A scientist must also be a poet"

Professor Alfred Kastler, 78, was awarded the Nobel Prize in Physics in 1966 after a lifetime of teaching and research. He believes that science can be both a blessing and a danger to humankind.

Professor Kastler is a modest, unassuming man. As he opens the front door of his fifth-floor apartment in the Latin Quarter of Paris, he apologizes for the fact that he is wearing slippers with his well-cut gray suit. His drawing-room is dominated by a grand piano and a harp. Although he plays neither, he loves music.

My schooling included the rather weird experience of having to change from my own German language to French when I was sixteen years old. You see, I was born at Guebwiller in Alsace. This region was annexed by France in 1648, ceded to Germany from 1871 until 1918, when it became French again. So I started studying in German and ended in French. But I don't think this did me any harm.

My father was a tradesman, and none of my family were particularly brainy. I was about fourteen when my teachers – who were excellent, by the way – noticed that I had a gift for mathematics.

The École Normale Supérieure is one of Europe's foremost centers for the training of scientists.

This enabled me to obtain a scholarship to the École Normale Supérieure in Paris – the leading center for budding scientists, and one of Europe's finest Institutes. A year later, in 1922, I was privileged to meet Albert Einstein on his first visit to Paris from Berlin. It's strange to recall that he was unpopular in those days as he was looked on as a German, and of course the First World War had only just ended. Einstein had been awarded the Nobel Prize in Physics the year before, at the age of forty-two. By the way, I was sixty-four when I was awarded mine.

After receiving my science degree, I taught until 1945. I spent most of World War II at the École Normale Supérieure. Another teacher there at that time was Georges Pompidou, who later became president of France. Obviously little research could be done during the war, so I had to wait until afterwards to build up a research team of ten students to work in my specialized field – the structure of the atom, which should not be confused with nuclear bombs.

I didn't expect to receive the Nobel Prize. The first hint that I might be awarded it came from a Swedish journalist on the evening before the announcement; he told me that I was on the list. The cash prize was worth 28,000 pounds, (about $44,000) at the time. It's worth more today.

Did the prize affect my life? It's a heavy burden in many ways, because there's a continual call on my time for interviews, or on my support for petitions. I have to refuse many of them.

Many people believe that scientific discoveries come only from hard, logical, reasoned thought. That is so, but it's important to remember that intuition

This equipment is destined for one of France's nuclear power plants.

also plays a part. A scientist must also be a poet. In mathematics there is also poetry.

Do I think that any of my work has helped us to understand the universe? No, I don't think so. But the role of science in the world is vital, for good or evil. I believe science has been positive in improving our life, especially in the field of communications. But it is also the cause of a major danger – nuclear war.

"We grumble but we're flourishing"

Roger Challier, 55, has a 50-hectare (125-acre) pig farm with some cattle, near Strasbourg. It is an average-sized farm in France. The French farmer does not give too much thought to the policies of the Common Market.

I like growing things, but I like animals as well, and my farm combines both. It's what you call a mixed farm. I have about 1,000 pigs for fattening and selling to pork butchers, and ninety sows for breeding purposes. Pigs are funny animals. They're highly intelligent, but people don't believe it because of their snouts. They can also be vicious, and will sometimes eat their young. I know of a case when a woman was knocked off her bicycle by three pigs and they killed and half ate her. They're incredibly strong.

We have twenty milking cows here – Friesians – which feed off the grassland which is unsuitable for cultivation. There is also arable land, as you can see, where I grow mainly corn and barley

The French eat so much pork that they have to import it to augment their own production.

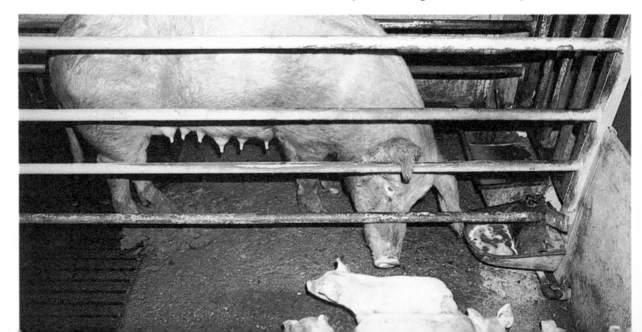

for pig fodder. During the war city folk collected edible waste such as cabbage cores and potato peelings, and we farmers collected it once a week for our pigs. There's terrible waste these days, you know. Anyway my pigs get the best fodder now and pork butchers get the tastiest meat.

I was born on this farm, which was run by my father. I was never sure whether I wanted to be a farmer myself, but then the war broke out when I was fourteen and so I really had no choice. By the end of the war I was nineteen and I just stayed on until I came to like it.

The farm is big enough for two families. My son and his wife also live here and I have another son who has a farm similar to mine quite nearby. My wife and daughter-in-law work about three hours a day on the farm itself in addition to their domestic work. My son and I work about ten hours a day, or throughout the daylight hours.

I don't know much about this European Common Market. There are supposed to be huge farm surpluses but we French don't care about that. We would sooner have too much stored away than starve. And people did starve in the war you know. How can anybody forget that?

I suppose the Common Market would be fine if only we exported our pork, but the French are so fond of pork that we import it. In Normandy there's the famous "Valley of the Pigs" where half a million are reared, probably the biggest concentration of them anywhere in Europe. There just can't be enough pigs in this country. That's why we have so many kinds of sausages. Have you ever known a country with so many sausages? It's the best food in the world.

There are no daily milk deliveries nor

Charcuteries offer a wide variety of cold meat delicacies.

any "milk marketing board," mainly because the French are not milk-minded, but also because French farmers don't accept organized markets easily.

There are about 17 million hectares (42 million acres) of cultivated land in France and 13 million hectares (32 million acres) of pastureland, 14 million hectares (34 million acres) of woods and forests, and 1.3 million hectares (3.2 million acres) of vineyards. About 8 million hectares (20 million acres) are uncultivated.

This means that France is, apart from Spain, the only Western European country which can grow all its own food.

There are big government subsidies for what is termed "income support". In general, French farmers, despite their grumbling, are flourishing.

Vacations are not for me. I hate leaving the farm, and I have all my committees to attend as well. I'm vice-chairman of the local farmers' union and member of half a dozen agricultural commissions. Almost half my time is spent on them, so where would I find time for vacations?

"No strikes without good reason"

Claude Jenet, 39, is a member of the 12-man ruling council of the one-million-strong Force Ouvrière trade union, one of France's "big three." He is proud of the benefits which trade unions have brought to his countrymen.

I suppose I was destined to become a trade union leader. My father was always talking about unions and I come from Limoges in central France, which has a long tradition of workers fighting for their rights in the shoe, furniture, printing and porcelain factories there.

I was nineteen when I joined the Force Ouvrière (F.O.). It was founded in 1948 after a split in the Communist-led General Confederation of Labor (C.G.T.).

I held a number of jobs in small firms and became a civil servant in the financial section, always organizing my colleagues. Then I was made a full-time F.O. delegate at Paris headquarters.

Today my official title is Confederation Secretary responsible for Press Relations – putting the F.O. on the mass media map. We also have our own weekly and monthly publications.

There's a lot of traveling involved, not only abroad – I've just returned from West Germany and the United States – but also throughout France, keeping in touch with all our 13,000 branches.

We're growing monthly. I think this is mainly because we're non-Communist and we stress the role of negotiation in labor disputes. We don't call our workers

Force Ouvrière is a bastion of the non-Communist left. This is its headquarters.

Trade union activities often lead to a mass rally if workers do not get their demands.

out on strike without good reason.

We've taken a leading part in limiting the working week to forty hours, obtaining a month's paid vacation a year, and also additional retirement benefits. All an F.O. member has to pay as his monthly union dues is the equivalent of one hour's pay. He gets a bargain.

Our problems have changed in the past five years. Today they include two new factors – robots and computers. We have to safeguard the jobs of our members, and yet we must show we aren't against progress. After all, they said the steam engine was harmful 150 years ago. We mustn't make a stand against modern-day "steam engines."

We also face some strange labor paradoxes these days. For example, a man gets paid more according to his qualifications. In other words, the more specialized he is, the better off he is – or was in the old days. But we've found that the greater his specialization, the sooner a man is out of a job because technical progress advances so fast.

France is probably the least trade-union-minded country in Europe, with only about twenty-five percent of the work force organized. Yet unions have brought massive benefits, starting in 1936 with the paid week's annual vacation. There were none before. Today it has gone up to one month.

Most workers have a forty-hour week, and now we're planning a thirty-five-hour week.

French workers have also won agreements guaranteeing them their pay for one year after they've lost their jobs through the economic recession. The first time in the history of the working class movement anywhere in the world that it has obtained such an agreement.

Unemployment benefits are paid partly by the state, and the balance is made up by employers and workers in a four-to-one ratio. After a year on full pay, a worker is paid a percentage until he finds a job.

"Perfume – a major growth industry"

Charlette Lelan, 32, has her own perfume shop in Nice, on the Côte d'Azur. In spite of the fact that the perfume industry is one of France's major export successes, only one French woman in ten ever goes into a *parfumerie*.

I opened this little shop three years ago when I discovered that, although this is one of the longest and busiest streets in Nice, it did not have a single *parfumerie* (perfume shop). Bookshops, bistros, laundries and groceries – yes, but a *parfumerie* – no.

I'll never forget those first few weeks: not a single customer. But then my first customer came in, rather shyly, and I

The center of the French perfume industry is found in the small town of Grasse, near Cannes.

A "nose" tests a perfume before it is bottled. Most "noses" are men.

made my first sale. On the average I have about twenty-five customers a day, which is considered extremely good for a one-woman *parfumerie* like mine.

Of course, perfume is expensive. The largest bottle called a *flacon* is one ounce. The smallest is one-quarter ounce. They cost anything between 240 francs ($33) and 595 francs ($83).

I'll let you in on a secret which is almost unbelievable for France: only ten women out of 100 ever enter a *parfumerie*.

Some of those ninety think they can't afford perfume, and a few count on their husbands to buy it for them. But the vast majority are afraid of being criticized for the makeup they are wearing. For perfume is all part of the beautifying process.

As you know it is one of France's major growth industries. French perfume is exported to over 100 foreign countries.

I'm always being asked why we charge so much for perfume. The ingredients are rare and costly like attar of roses, which comes from a valley in Bulgaria, and musk from certain mammals, or ambergris from sperm whales. The scent must attract, but also cling and not evaporate too quickly.

I can't think of a more pleasant life for a woman than being surrounded by perfumes. I'm not at all tired when I get home to look after my children. Even they have their own perfumes – we start early in France.

Although perfume is such a feminine product, they are all made to formulas approved by a person called in the trade a "nose." And those "noses" are all male. They are the final arbiter of a new scent, one more male bastion in a woman's world. But one day a female "nose" will appear on the scene. Maybe me. Who knows?

"Improved status for French women"

Elizabeth Roy, 30, lives in a rented apartment in Rennes with her husband and their three children. Although her life revolves around her home and family, she welcomes the improved status that women have gained in French society.

I have very little leisure time. I'm always first up in the mornings, and then I must get Yann and Gaelle ready for school. Jennifer is only five months old, but she joins the family for breakfast at 7:30 a.m.

Breakfast is always coffee – chocolate drink for the children – toast and jam. No newspapers at the table. Believe it or not, this is the only meal we have together as a family during the week. My husband gets back to the apartment about 8:00 p.m. and by then the children have been bathed and put to bed. Our only other meals together are on weekends. Then I cook something special and we relax together as a family.

The children are off to school early. Yann no longer needs me to take him to his nearby primary school and Gaelle shares a carpool set up with my neighbors. Then I sort out what has to be done that day.

The routine hardly ever changes. There's the washing, ironing, and shopping to do, and before I know where I am it's 11:30 a.m. and the children are back

for their lunch. Lunch is usually a first course such as grated carrots, followed by mashed potatoes with perhaps a pork chop or hamburger, and then cheese and yoghurt to finish.

Shopping has become difficult for the housewife who has to count her francs. And most of us have to nowadays. About once every two weeks I go to a supermarket to stock up with the main items,

Supermarkets such as this one are putting many small grocery stores out of business.

but we have small stores in the neighborhood where I buy basic groceries, milk, and bread, which I buy fresh every day.

I even get meat and fish at the supermarket. Both have become enormously expensive. We buy a lot of pork and beef – at about 35 francs a kilo ($2.20 a lb). Lamb is really too expensive and I don't buy veal. There was a scare recently; apparently farmers inject their calves with large amounts of hormones to make them grow faster, so I joined the veal boycott and have just not gone back to buying it again.

My husband often joins me on a Sunday morning in going to a local, open-air market. That's where you can find the best bargains – cheeses, eggs, meat, fish, fruit and vegetables.

A typical Sunday lunch would be a first course of pâté with tomato salad, then roast pork or beef, potatoes and beans or peas, followed by a choice of fresh cheeses with a lettuce salad, ice-cream and coffee. My husband buys our wine – usually an inexpensive red. When we have an anniversary or birthday to celebrate we buy oysters or snails

Housewives can still find bargains at local open-air food markets.

or frogs' legs, and then of course we have a more expensive wine.

We can't really go out in the evening because of the children. Baby-sitters are hard to find. I like to go to the local center where we paint or sew and discuss books we're reading.

The status of women has improved enormously in France recently. Valéry Giscard d'Estaing, who was president before Mitterand, created the Ministry for Women's Status. The minister was France's leading magazine editor, Françoise Giroud. There is a vast inequality between men and women as far as employment is concerned, and Mme. Giroud prophesied that "full equality," where women earn the same as men for the same work, will take a generation.

Women teachers and bank clerks all get about twenty percent less than men doing the same jobs, and during an economic recession women are the first to be dismissed.

In 1981 the first woman was elected to the Académie Française – the "Forty Immortals" – founded in 1635. She was the author Marguerite Yourcenar.

"Lack of money hampers archaeology"

Jean-Christophe Galipaud, 25, is a student at the Faculty of Arts and Archaeology in Paris. Although France is rich in undiscovered treasures, little money and few facilities are afforded to archaeologists.

In 1973 I went to study archaeology for three years at Cologne University in West Germany. At that time, it was impossible to study that subject by itself at a French university; it had to be combined with the history of art. That has changed today. But what has not changed is the fact that while there are tens of thousands of scholarships in France for all kinds of studies, there is not a single one for archaeology.

I have to work at any job that I can get, so I can earn enough money to study at the Faculty of Archaeology here, where the dean is José Garanger, France's leading specialist in Oceanian prehistory.

There are only ten students at the faculty taking archaeology; the rest are studying the History of Art. In the whole

A student band raises funds and brings unexpected amusement to Paris shoppers.

of France, which is rich in prehistoric "digs," there are only 200 students and four major archaeological faculties.

Of course, there's wide interest in the subject and many amateur associations. But few professionals, such as I hope to become, devote their entire life to the subject.

It's true that there are not many jobs available in this field. I find it strange that there are such treasures to uncover, and yet so little money is available to find them.

I suppose France's most prestigious prehistoric site must be the paintings of animals in the Lascaux Grottoes. There must be many more sites. But there are only about eight digs going on at present in the whole country: lack of archaeologists due to lack of money.

I'm always meeting people who ask what's the point of searching around old places where people lived 50,000 years ago. But surely it's fascinating to know about our ancestors. For instance, at present I'm studying one of man's most enormous steps forward – his use of fire. It meant cooked food, and better health and a longer life, and also warm caves and buildings which improved living conditions and led to an increase in population. I'm amused sometimes when I hear people grumble about their living conditions – all they have to do for light and warmth is flick a switch.

So far as I know, there are no digs available for students this year. But last year a fellow student went to Tahiti to study ancient fishing techniques.

You have to know something about everything in archaeology. You must be able to draw, and have a knowledge of mathematics and geometry, logic and, of course, be capable of hard physical work.

Students relax at a Latin-Quarter bistro, where they can spend more time than money.

There's too much ignorance about archaeology these days, and this often leads to the destruction of valuable sites. When we first arrive at a new site, we're welcomed with open arms, but that doesn't last long. The local farmers soon realize that they won't be able to use the land on which we're searching.

Ignorance, occasional open hostility, lack of money – nothing will stop me. There are so many treasures in France alone just waiting to be uncovered. And so few of us to do it.

There are over 750,000 students at twenty-four universities, and over 25,000 at the Paris Sorbonne alone. They're divided into the main faculties of law, economics, medicine, science, letters, pharmacy and technology.

In Paris, the Latin Quarter, which dates from the twelfth century, has long been the traditional haunt of students. Here they can sit for hours in cafés. At the age of eighteen, Françoise Sagan wrote her best-seller *Bonjour Tristesse (Hello Sadness)* here. But archaeology has yet to be "discovered" by the students.

"My position brings no perks"

Jacques Reynault, 40, is a man of the future who seems more at home in the year 2,000 than today. He works as a manager in a company that produces pharmaceutical products.

I manage a staff of 250 men and women. We're carrying out work in new fields that didn't even exist ten years ago. Bio-chemistry is a modern growth industry and it's developing as fast as the computer industry did fifteen years ago.

All you see is gleaming, highly-complicated machinery, and men and women in white smocks; it makes the factory seem like a hospital.

We make antibiotics here, as well as vitamins and enzymes, by a process of mass fermentation. These are lifesaving medicines, and we have to mass-produce them as cheaply as possible. We really are in the business of lifesaving.

I don't come from this region, but from the south. I went to school in Marseilles and then went to Paris to study for a

French people often spend a fortune when they visit the drugstore.

degree at the National Institute of Agronomy.

Then I worked four years in a research laboratory in Switzerland, and after that for ten months in a laboratory in the United States. Then I came back to France to work for this company. I have been here ten years.

There's a lot of work to be done, and my day lasts from 7:45 a.m. to 6:00 p.m. with just thirty minutes off for lunch. Managers, even in France, no longer have time for those three-hour lunches you read about.

Yes, like most managers these days, I take work home on weekends. Unfortunately, my job is almost all paperwork, but at least at home I can relax and enjoy doing it.

I also have to keep abreast of developments by reading technical journals and magazines. Usually I read them from 6:45 a.m. to 9:00 a.m. on Saturdays and Sundays.

I live in a small town not far from here. Because I know all the shortcuts and back roads, I don't lose much time traveling to and from work.

I like my work and enjoy working for a company where I feel I can make a contribution. In return I expect the company to contribute to my well-being with a good salary, and good working conditions.

I consider I'm well paid. I receive a monthly salary but no more benefits than any other worker here. We all have health insurance and pension plans and an annual vacation with pay, but I don't get any special extras because of my position.

Until last year, I used to play volley ball in a team every Sunday afternoon and alternate Saturdays. We all used to

The complex equipment used in a modern bio-chemical factory.

go together as a family and the boys played too. Now I'm too old for that, and my main sporting activity is tennis, which is easier to fit in with my other commitments.

People in key managerial positions – referred to as *cadres* in France – clearly have the advantage in keeping their jobs when a recession hits their industry. They're the "hire-and-fire" men and as such are the last to go.

But a big danger is that some *cadres* are so highly specialized that once they are amongst the jobless, they find it difficult to find jobs to fit their qualifications.

In addition, the powerful French *Patronat*, or Association of Employers, makes special financial provisions for out-of-work *cadres*, usually guaranteeing education for their children and helping with mortgage payments.

"Exploitation by the businessmen"

Dr. Jean Malaurie is the world's leading expert on Eskimos. Head of research at the National Center of Scientific Research, he has recently finished filming Eskimo civilizations for a seven-part television series.

Dr. Malaurie is a tall and powerful figure, a human dynamo, whose book-lined study has so many furs that it looks like a trapper's hut in the Far North.

Eskimos don't like being called by that word, which they consider downgrading (it means eater of raw meat) but prefer the word Inuit.

There are 100,000 of them living in Greenland (the largest island in the world), Canada, Alaska and Soviet Eastern Siberia. I've just finished filming the Inuit civilization, which is on its way to being ruined by Western progress. It took me five months to film these four communities and two years to edit the film for a seven-part television series. I used three seven-man teams to cover Inuits in Greenland (where there are 50,000); Alaska (30,000); Northeastern Canada (24,000); and Siberia (1,500).

The Inuits originally came from China 10,000 years ago and spread over the Far North.

Today they are suffering from Western progress — or modern civilization — which has brought alcoholism, drugs, unemployment and mental illness.

The new generation of Inuits can't even build an igloo. They are like boy scouts who have forgotten how to tie knots or light fires.

It may sound strange, but the four Eskimo communities had never had any communication before I organized the First Inuit Conference, in Rouen in northern France, in 1973. It was backed by the late Réné Cassin, France's Nobel Peace

Survival is not easy in the harsh conditions of the North Pole.

Traditions survive, but Western progress has brought many problems to the Inuits.

Prize winner who wrote the *Human Rights Charter* for the United Nations.

I've been told that in some places schools teach that the Eskimo (Inuit) language has no word for war, as they are such peaceful people. This is not true. In fact, they're very aggressive, otherwise they would never survive the harsh climate at the North Pole.

In Siberia I met Inuits living in the coldest place in the world with average temperatures of −60°C (−76°F) and only three hours of daylight.

Seventy families live by hunting in an area as large as two or three French *départements*. They've been a nation of hunters for thousands of years. When the Thule community was discovered by accident in 1918, they had never seen either wood or metal.

Today they ride around in jeeps and helicopters and live in prefabricated houses sent to them in ships.

They are being exploited by the Western businessman, among others. Take an example. Beautiful pelts and furs which they bring to trading posts are bought for next to nothing, then sold at high prices in the West.

An Inuit told me: "We are nobody. We have lost our language, hunting grounds and way of life. We are nothing."

But there are positive factors. The first Inuit university has been built at Port Barrow, Alaska. The Ice People are beginning to understand how to deal with the invading whites, and their population has doubled in the past 100 years.

I started my scientific career as a geologist and concentrated on deserts, especially the Sahara, and tundra regions.

Now I study the peoples in a region of icebergs and glaciers. That's where I want to be buried.

"It's harder to make ends meet"

Odile Laug works as a free-lance nurse in Pau, specializing in giving shots at home or in her small office. The work is hard and ill paid. French doctors believe that treatment by injection is the most effective method of introducing medicine into the patient's system.

I'm a state registered nurse; I've worked in major hospitals in England, Switzerland and in Paris. There's one big difference between French medical treatment and that in other European countries, and that's the doctor's reliance on a series of injections. That leaves room for somebody like me who can build up her own private business treating patients who have to have daily shots over a period of weeks.

But it's tough. To make a living I must see between thirty and forty patients a day, and I have to make personal calls at the homes of about twenty of them.

I work a twelve-hour day, starting at 8:00 a.m. Of course, I must also be ready to deal with emergencies and to work on Sundays.

I used to go out at night to patients' homes, but it has become too dangerous. One of my colleagues was attacked and had to have thirty-two stitches in her head and face. So I refuse to make night calls. Drug addicts can be dangerous as they think nurses carry drugs on them.

Actually we don't but they don't know this.

There's lots of work for me in this district, which has about a dozen doctors. This residential area was built in about 1932, when young married couples came to live here. Today they're in their seven-

ties or older. One is 100. So they need a lot of injections.

Fortunately modern technical progress has come to my rescue by inventing a throwaway plastic syringe and needle. They cost only one franc (14¢) each, and this saves me coming home and spending two hours sterilizing the old metal ones we used.

It's getting harder and harder for freelance nurses to make ends meet. Three of my colleagues in this area have quit. I believe 2,000 throughout France left last year.

Of course, the work itself must be a vocation. But it's hard – I have to deal with patients ranging from babies to the very old.

The injections have to be deep, up to four centimeters into a muscle, so a nurse has to have a nice bedside manner. Because the shots are so deep, the medicine penetrates speedily and effec-

A large proportion of Odile's patients are older people who require constant medical attention.

One of Europe's most modern hospitals, the Bichat, in Paris.

tively throughout the body. The French are great believers in the needle, unlike the Americans, for instance.

There are an estimated 100,000 doctors in France and 34,000 pharmacists. But there's a big private health sector; there are about 380,000 state hospital beds compared with 180,000 beds in private clinics.

Basically the French want to feel that there's always the state health service to look after them. But if they wish, they can use the private sector – if they have the money.

Nurses in France don't wear uniforms as they do in America and Switzerland, for example. I suppose it's part of a Frenchwoman's character not to be too regimented. Some private hospitals insist on white blouses, skirts and dresses, but they never resemble a uniform.

But, frankly, I like the smart turnout of a nurse's uniform.

55

"The creative mind is still in France"

Julien Porisse, 53, lives and paints in the heartland of the French art world – the Place du Tertre, in Montmartre. He believes that Paris is still where you find the great creative artists of the world.

I suppose I'm the luckiest man in the world – an artist who has his own gallery from which to sell his paintings.

I should have gone into the centuries-old family textile business, but at the age of six I was taken to England and only returned to France after the war. So my English is as good as my French. My mother hated England and was delighted to buy a house here just beside the Place du Tertre for the ridiculous sum of 10,000 francs ($1,400). Today it's my art gallery, which I opened in 1963. My mother, by the way, is hale and hearty and lives on the Riviera, painting like me.

During the war there were few art instructors in schools so, as I was a gifted artist, I did some teaching. Generally speaking of course, drawing and painting can't be learned – either the talent is there or it isn't. You can teach pupils to improve and, of course, you can teach art history, one of the most fascinating subjects in the world.

I suppose in some ways I'm a living witness to the history of art. I can speak for hours on Utrillo, for instance, who lived and worked here for decades. Do you know that there are supposed to be 75,000 authenticated Utrillos in the world. Of course, that cannot be true. Many of these pictures are forgeries. I knew a man with a furniture shop here

The Beaubourg Center near Notre Dame contains some of the world's finest art.

Painting tourists' portraits is a year-round job for the artists in Montmartre's Place du Tertre.

who gave away free Utrillos to every customer who bought a "suite" of furniture.

And he neglected to keep one himself – after all he was only paying a few francs at the time and didn't put any value on them. That's the art world for you.

Don't believe stories about starving artists. We're always told how badly Michelangelo was treated by the Pope over payment for the Sistine Chapel, but you know he received twice as much as the cost of the biggest ship in Genoa harbor.

Van Gogh: his trouble wasn't poverty – he had a regular if small income from his brother Theo. His problem was a total inability to communicate with other people. That's why he committed suicide. It had nothing to do with money.

Paris is still the art capital of the world: there's something about the atmosphere of the place, its people and architecture. There are higher prices being paid in New York and Tokyo, but the creative mind is in France.

The world's newest art museum is the Beaubourg Center near Notre Dame Cathedral; it was built to honor President Georges Pompidou. Some people think the outside looks like an oil refinery, but inside you can see some of the finest art in the world. Not so long ago even kings weren't as lucky as the ordinary person today seeking to study art.

There are three kinds of art buyers: the investors, who see paintings as though they are stock certificates; the collectors, who might just as well be in stamps or pottery; and then the ordinary buyer, the man or woman who likes what he or she sees.

The biggest price that I've ever obtained was 10,000 francs ($1,400) for two lithographs by Toulouse-Lautrec. But money is not wealth: wealth is ideas and creative work.

Yes, it's true some artists are eccentrics. Like my dear friend Gaston Tyko who went by train from Paris to Rome dressed in a centurion's armor. He was arrested. The police thought he was crazy. He committed suicide in Tokyo. If you see any of his works, here is a tip – buy.

"A mayor must be a leader"

Jean Tricart, 65, is mayor of Poissy, a small industrial town. He is a former deputy of the National Assembly. The two main problems he has to deal with are housing and unemployment.

The mayor has to do everything in a town, including many things he shouldn't have to do. You're in contact with people every day. Recently, a mother of four children was evicted from her apartment and came to me. I gave her 200 francs ($28) from my special fund for such cases. But there are happy occasions as well. One of my jobs is to officiate at civil weddings. In France there's always a civil ceremony in the town hall.

I don't do many of them these days, as I leave the more enjoyable tasks to my two deputy mayors.

The mayor and his council work under the guidance of the *préfet*, an official who represents the government in Paris. But when it comes to making decisions here in Poissy, I don't have

When the Talbot factory sneezes, Poissy catches a cold.

to get the approval of Pierre or Paul somewhere else in France. I'm independent.

A mayor has to be a leader; if he isn't, he'll make a bad mayor. I was elected for six years. Many mayors in France are also regional councillors and representatives but I don't like that idea because you're constantly pulled this way and that way by conflicting interests. But before I became mayor I was representative for the Haute-Vienne, in Western France.

I have two main problems, probably like most mayors: unemployment and housing. You see, French mayors are different from those in many countries. I'm not just a figurehead. I'm an executive official, more like the American mayor, and I have to make day-to-day decisions.

Poissy is a heavily built-up industrial center with a large car factory – Talbot – employing 23,000 workers along the Seine valley. We say that when this factory sneezes, Poissy catches a cold. If the factory starts laying off workers, that cuts right through our society here. And jobs are not easy to find these days. So unemployment is a major worry.

Then there's the housing shortage. It's caused because we are not a large town. But, because people want to live near their work, we've become involved in vast building projects to provide comfortable homes at reasonable rents – easy to say, but difficult to achieve.

We have either to find a developer or to form a joint company with a private firm. Then we must get approval from the department for planning. Of course, we have to raise the cash, usually through bank loans, and as they charge high interest, we have to charge higher rents than we would like. But without the loans there would be no houses – a vicious circle.

The town hall, and that is me, also has to look after the nursery and primary schools. The state pays the teachers, but we have to provide premises and equipment. We've made a special effort for our tiny tots, and there are many of them because in this town there's a large immigrant population with big families. We have had to start special language classes. We even have a farm where the children go with their teachers for one week every year to learn about the countryside and breathe in some fresh air.

Sorry, but I have to go now. Something's wrong with a sewer somewhere, and then I have to return for a council meeting. My time seems to be spent answering a whole lot of questions – like yours, for example.

But that's service, and a mayor has to give service above all.

Mayors in France are responsible for such day-to-day problems as road repairs and sewerage works.

"French banks have more imagination"

Claude Lemaire, 36, is the manager of a branch of Banque Populaire (B.I.C.S.) on the capital's famous Boulevard Saint Michel. The standing of French banks, he feels, is greatly underestimated in world banking circles.

I'm not at all sure that the world gives France enough credit for its banking system. Do you know that a list of the world's biggest banks was drawn up recently, and to the surprise of many, the number one bank with the biggest assets was a French bank – Crédit Agricole. In fact, there were four French banks in the top ten major world banks. The Americans and the English nearly had a fit.

France went through a banking revolution in the period from 1965 to 1967, when branches were opened hastily everywhere. This place used to be a family grocer, and two doors away there is another bank which used to be a bakery. I opened this branch nine years ago, and today we handle 3,000 accounts.

We specialize in helping the small businessman and the worker, who fifteen years ago would never have dreamed of using a checkbook. Everybody has a checkbook these days, but the worst fears of the pessimists about bad checks have never been realized.

B.I.C.S. handled 14.5 million checks last year and of these a mere 6,700 were duds.

The French are overwhelmingly honest, although strict banking laws also help to keep them on the right track.

The French bank seems to operate with more speed and imagination than

The original shareholders of the Banque de France met in the sumptuous Galerie Dorée.

some of its foreign counterparts. Credit is much easier here. We would never refuse to lend a man the equivalent of his monthly salary. Then we have an enormous number of additional services. These include travel insurance, obtaining theater tickets, and buying stocks and gold with the help of our experts.

I became a banker absolutely by chance. After I graduated from school I was uncertain what to do, so became a bank clerk. Mind you I was strong in mathematics. But these days with computers even this isn't essential for a bank manager. With eight years' experience I was made manager here, and I've stayed here ever since.

I'm not sure that the old French saying "as safe as a bank" is all that true today. The danger of a holdup is a real one. The bank next door has been held up twice, and we ourselves were attacked by three masked gunmen eighteen months ago.

I was on the telephone speaking to my wife and just managed to tell her there was a holdup when a hooded man appeared at my office door with his gun pointed straight between my eyes.

Frankly I was paralyzed with fear and so were the rest of my staff. One gunman jumped over the bulletproof window, which strangely enough didn't reach to the ceiling, and stole 17,000 francs ($2,300). They were out in the street within two minutes. Ten minutes later the police arrived – held up in heavy traffic. The gunmen have never been caught.

I spend so much time in this office that I've make it comfortable with plants, modern paintings on the wall and indirect lighting. When clients come in with their financial problems and go out happier, you know how I feel? – like a doctor who has eased their money "ills." Call me Dr. Lemaire!

These vaults keep safe France's gold reserves which total some 26 million francs ($3.6 million).

Facts

Capital city: Paris.

Principal language: French with numerous regional dialects. Small minorities speak Breton or Basque.

Currency: French franc = 100 centimes and is worth about 14 U.S. cents.

Religion: No religion is officially recognized by the state, but, of the total population, 45.3 million are Roman Catholics, 2 million are Moslems and 750,000 are Protestants.

Population: 54,000,000 (1982). Only 70 percent of the French population live in towns. Cities are overcrowded. France has an unusually high proportion of both young and elderly people.

Climate: Temperate, except in the south where it is Mediterranean, and in the northwest where it is oceanic.

Government: France has a bicameral parliament. The Senate has 295 members indirectly elected for 9 years. The National Assembly has 491 members directly elected by universal adult suffrage for 5 years. Executive power is held by the President of the Republic who is elected by direct universal suffrage every 7 years. He nominates the Prime Minister and other government members and appoints military and civil offices. France is divided into 21 administrative regions containing 98 metropolitan departments, with a prefect and an elected council. There are also 5 overseas departments and 5 overseas territories. The district (arrondissement) has an elected council. The canton comprises about 10 communes. The unit of local government is the commune. A municipal council controls the affairs of the commune. The mayor is elected by the municipal council. He represents the council and is the agent of central government at the local level.

Housing: There has been a housing crisis since the Second World War. One-third of all dwellings are over 100 years old.

Education: Education is compulsory and free for children aged 6–16 years. About one in five pupils are privately educated, mostly in Roman Catholic institutions. There is noncompulsory preschool instruction for children aged 2–5 years; compulsory elementary instruction for children aged 6–11 years (primary schools and lycées); and secondary education for children aged 11–18 years. The first secondary cycle is a 4-year general course. At 15, children proceed to the second cycle, choosing between the longer option leading to the baccalauréat, or the short cycle with commercial, administrative or industrial options. France has 62 universities; 6 university centers; and 3 national polytechnic institutes.

Military service: Military service is compulsory and lasts 1 year. Draft age is 19 years.

Agriculture: France is largely self-supporting in food. Main crops: wheat, sugarbeets and barley. Despite a movement away from the land, agriculture still plays an important role in the French economy.

Industry: Main industries: engineering, chemicals, textiles, food and construction. France has fewer large companies than most other major Western European countries.

Media: There are more than 100 daily newspapers in France, of which only one, L'Humanité, is the mouthpiece for a political party (Communist). There are 7 state-financed broadcasting companies – 3 television channels and 4 radio stations. There are also 9 regional and 21 local radio stations.

Family spending: In 1978 the average French family income was spent as follows: food – 21.1 percent; fuel and power – 8.5 percent; manufactured goods – 31.6 percent; and services – 37.8 percent, including rent – 9.8 percent; health – 9.5 percent; and transport and telecommunications – 2.9 percent.

Index

Glossary

apéritif A drink, usually wine, drunk before a meal to whet the appetite.

baguette A long, narrow, stick-shaped loaf of French bread.

bistro A small restaurant.

boulevard A wide, usually tree-lined, road in a city.

cadres Management positions in French business and industry.

cave A wine cellar, (pronounced "kahv").

Champs Elysées A famous, broad and tree-lined avenue in Paris, noted for its elegance.

Côte d'Azur ("The Azure Coast") Southeastern France on the Mediterranean; part of the Riviera.

cuisine A style or manner of cooking. It also means a kitchen or cooking department.

département One of 95 administrative areas into which France is divided (not counting four overseas *départements*). The central government appoints the prefects who administer the *départements*.

gendarme A state trooper.

guillotine An instrument of execution consisting of a weighted blade set between two posts.

hors d'oeuvre A dish served as an appetizer, usually before the main meal.

parfumerie A store where perfume is sold.

prima donna A temperamental person.